CW00864449

The Art of Effective Communication In A Digital World

By Donna Still

Cover Design: Donna Still www.donnastill.com
Book Design: Ultimate Life Publishing,
www.donnastill.com
Book Production: Create Space an www.amazon.com
company

Legal Disclaimer

Dedication

To my dearest husband and partner in life, Alan without whom none of this would ever have been conceived let alone written.
Thank you from the most deepest place in my heart x

The Art of Effective Communication In A Digital World

By Donna Still

Why is this book important now?

In todays fast paced digital world effective communication skills are even more important than any other time in history. The leadership roles don't necessarily go to the person with the best technical know-how, they tend to go to the people who can confidently and effectively communicate and share their ideas. The higher earning potential always follows the people who can arouse enthusiasm in others and assume leadership using great communication skills. Oftentimes the best Leaders Are Effective Communicators. They understand others and get along with people; they are quickly able to build trusting relationships where everyone wins.

Our current economic and market trends are driving many to want to get more done with less resources and to add to that, people generally don't have time to listen or wait. Much of today's communication is now delivered via digital methods, even if the people are sitting just a few feet away. So, just how does one communicate more effectively ensuring that others understand exactly what you mean the first time?

This book will take you through the crucial elements and secrets of effective communication, that when applied will ensure you get what you want when you want and have others saying yes more easily. Good communications are the foundation on which all-personal relationships; great companies and successful careers are built and are vital to positively impact all areas of your life.

In this digital age there's no shortage of ways for us to communicate and interact with any one from any where in the world. The challenge happens when we meet another face to face and we must find the right words to say and communicate them in the right way. By the end of this book you will have a tool set of skills that will enable you to always be in control of any situation and communicate in the most effective way to connect and get the results you want so every one wins.

Objectives: By completing the exercises this book you will develop the skills to: -
- Enhance your communication efforts to make the most of leadership opportunities
- Improve your every day relationships, both personal and professional at all levels
- Get the results you want, with or without authority
- Feel more confident
- Improve your leadership skills

Outcomes:
By the end of this book you will:
- Understand how to communicate so others will feel at ease with you and want to help you
- Discover and be able to apply powerful language patterns that enable you to connect in a deeper more meaningful way, so that everyone wins
- Discover and be able to apply the secret motivators that give you instant leadership qualities that others admire
- Know how to Unlock the factors of influence that cause people to easily want to say yes to you

Foreword

In a world where the media of communication is constantly advancing, the ability to understand and to be understood is extremely challenging. For successful communication to take place there is a definite need to plan for the desired outcome, which can be achieved by creating awareness and adapting the *way* in which you communicate.

Throughout this book the objectives of communication are highlighted and then put in to practice with tools and worksheets that entice you to take action. It makes you think and positively question your own style. By following the steps that are clearly outlined it becomes possible to develop a persuasive and influencer style that can be adapted to any situation. The book will become your communicator companion and by following the steps and exercises you will learn how to observe, mirror and influence people through your body language and choice of words in a way they will resonate with.

The direct voice of the author encourages you to be accountable for your own development while encouraging you to push your own boundaries through constant learning, testing and practice. A must read for anyone who wants to become a charismatic and influential leader in their field.

Hilary Steel,
Editor of Kent women in Business Magazine.. Performance Speaker and Award Ceremony Host. www.hilarysteel.com

Introduction

Communication is one of those vital skills that are never consciously taught to us at school. We are all master communicators but the methods we use vary greatly as do the results. What if there was a way to understand others more easily, so we can help them understand us more effectively? That's what I believe communication is about. Firstly understanding others so we can then help them understand us better, it's a two way dance that has reciprocity built in.

Over the last 21 years I have done a lot of training in the area of communication. It all began when I was operating as a painter & decorator, I would take on work experience youngsters and then have to find a way to help them understand my instructions! Also in the course of my work, I sat with a lot of couples who had stupidly busy lifestyles and hardly ever saw each other for more than a few minutes a day as they passed each other in the hallway, like ships in the night. I felt like a marriage guidance counselor as they wrestled with each other's ideas of a great room scheme and come to some agreement on the type of finish they wanted.

I also experienced a similar challenge when working with commercial clients who had groups of stakeholders and decision makers who all needed to be in the room and come to some agreement about what work was to be carried out. And as you can imagine, I spent a lot of time negotiating between the parties and all I wanted to do was get on with my job of decorating. There came a time when I had to do something drastic, which turned out to be the best thing I ever did. For the next 10 years my decorating practice was filled with a waiting list of eager clients.

In 2010 I made a conscious choice to end the decorating and work full time teaching others how to build their business and communicate more effectively using their innate skills and talents. I focus 100% of my time assisting small business owners in developing their communication & leaderships skills using my proven system. A Six Step Business Development System I've come to call 'Diamondology.' This helps both in the day-to-day operations and in the marketing activities of any business.

The content set out in this book is the culmination of a lifetime of training and development and tailored specifically to help you achieve better results whether you run a business or are employed. If after completing the modules set out in the book you'd like to share the content with your team, I'm happy to work with your organisation to improve communication and leadership skills. I can be contacted at donna@donnastill.com to book an initial strategy call.

Here is what we'll be covering in each chapter

Chapter 1 ~ What Is Effective Communication?
- The 3 Keys to Effective Communication
- Types of communication
- How language is formed

Chapter 2 ~ Effective Communication Is So Much More Than Just Talking
- The dance of communication
- Understanding our own communication style and How we represent & store information
- Discovering the power of the senses and the 6 mental faculties to communicate effectively

Chapter 3 ~ The 7 Vital Components Of Effective Communication
- Understand and apply the 7 vital components of effective communication
- Understand the power of intention and interest in communication
- The importance of Individual motivation traits

Chapter 4 ~ Unlock The Power of Language For Effective Communication
- Understand How words change minds
- Discover How to motivate both Proactive or Reactive Individuals
- How to deal with Hot Buttons so every one wins

I wish you every success in completing this course and look forward to hearing about your successes too. I can be contacted by email donna@donnastill.com

How To Complete This Book

The way I suggest you complete this book is to work through each chapter sequentially. Each chapter contains an introduction that covers the foundation of what you'll learn in each of the chapter's content and is designed to lead you through the development and practice of a new skill set. You'll see throughout each chapter there are opportunities to immediately put the theory into practice via the, *'Practice Points.'* This is where you get to experience in real time the skills you are developing in the chapter and learn how to integrate them into your being.

You'll also see that at the end of each chapter there is a, *'Knowledge Quiz,'* for you to complete to check your understanding and a *'Learning Journal*,' to help you set goals, track your progress and continue your development beyond the parameters of this book. There is a set printable pdf docs available at www.donnastill.com/resources/AoEC

Chapter 1

What Is Effective Communication?

Chapter 1 ~ What is Effective Communication?

Aims of this chapter:
To help you develop an understanding and appreciation of what makes an Effective Communication and to help you develop the skills required to easily identify your own communication style.

Objectives of this module:
By the end of this module you should be able to...
- Identify the 3 key components of an effective communication
- Understand and appreciate how ones own language has been formed and which representation system is naturally expressed when communicating
- Enjoy the Practice Points and Complete the knowledge quiz to cement understanding

Go to the learning journal page for chapter 1. You'll find it at the rear of the book in section called 'Learning Journal,' and complete the first part. By doing this you are focusing your intention on the benefits you'll receive from completing the exercises, it's also a great way to integrate and consolidate what you're learning.

Introduction
So, to begin we require a working definition of what we mean by, 'Effective Communication,' so we can all meet our desired our outcomes for this book."

The word 'Communication' has its source in the Latin word 'Commuñicăre' meaning to share.

The word 'Effective' is applied to that which has the power to achieve a specified result.

Together as 'Effective Communication,' we can understand their meaning for the purpose of this book as,
"The intended ACT of successfully conveying meaning through a shared system of signs, symbols and rule structures culturally agreed so that a specific result is achieved."

A bit of a mouthful I agree so here's the non-academic version!!!

"Communication is a word that can best describe any interaction with another, this could be a casual conversation, persuading, teaching, negotiating or writing. A dynamic process that requires the involvement of at least two people."

Where are you now?
As with all progressive development and before we go any further, we need to know and understand where you believe you are currently in your level of communication skills and how effective you believe you are. The benefits of this are to get a really good idea of your current level of skill and ability in your communication efforts. It will give you a foundation on which to build your effective communication success toolkit. You'll be more easily able to focus your energy on developing the areas that are most important to you.

Circle of communication

Within your family, how effectively do you communicate with your Parents? Your Siblings if you have them? Your Children if you have them? And, your extended relations and family members?

Within your work setting, how effectively do you communicate with your colleagues? Your boss or superior if you have one? And your clients if you are client facing?

How would you rate your communication skills online on social media?
And, finally what about your offline social skills, how effectively do you feel you communicate with your peers when face-to-face?

What's your purpose?

There are as many reasons as there are people on this planet for completing this book. Just so that you have absolute clarity about why you are participating in this inquiry and developing your specific toolkit for effective communication. We'd like you to write out in detail the reasons why you feel it's important to you to develop your skills and become a more effective communicator.

What happens when we communicate?

When one person pays attention to another, they take in what the other person is saying and doing. This initiates a process of getting in touch with the originators own internal thoughts and feelings, which then drives a response. The other person pays attention to them and so a communication loop is formed. Each individual therefore, responds based on his or her own thoughts, ideas and current beliefs.

What this displays is, that there is so much more to any communication than the words we use. Even saying nothing at all is a method of communicating.

Professor Albert Mehrabian in 1970 showed through scientific study, that when communicating to a group of people, 55% of the impact is determined by your body language. Your body language is made up of postures, gestures, facial expressions and eye contact. This is known as non-verbal communication. 38% of the impact is determined by your tone of voice and only 7% by the actual words spoken. Clearly this may change in certain circumstances but it does seem that getting your point across is not so much what you say, but how you say it.

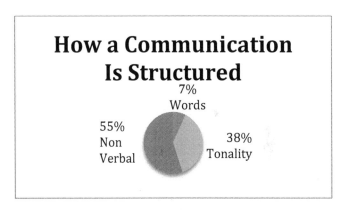

Practice Point 1
Think of a simple sentence – "my mum makes the best cakes."

Now say it over and over again six times, with the emphasis on a different word each time.
Notice now, how by changing the tone of your voice, loudness and timbre you can change the meaning.

Then add gestures, look up or look down, be still or active, breathe fast or slow, you get the message?

To change the ways in which you currently communicate, consider your body language, these include hand and feet gestures, volume, tone, pitch and rhythm of your voice along with the words you use.

The 3 Keys to Effective Communication

Now that you've had a chance to physically experience the results that a change of emphasis on the words has on an interaction, you will appreciate that the way you say something is just as important as what you say. Your body language and tonality has a profound impact on the messages you give out. There are 3 keys to an effective communication, they are

1. Your physiology – this is your body language,
2. Your psychology – which is your attitude or internal state and
3. Your language – which are the words and tonality you use.

Every communication is broadcasting exactly what is happening in your subconscious mind at every moment in relation to the three above areas.

How We Experience And Represent The World

As humans we take in our experiences through our senses and translate those experiences into thoughts. We have an incredible ability to use our thought processes to recreate sensory experiences internally. For example, when remembering something pleasant we smile. An unpleasant one will rekindle painful emotions; the thought of a favourite food will have us salivating.

We *represent* our experiences to ourselves using our senses, which in scientific terms is called, '*our*

20

representational system.' It is commonly agreed that there are 5 representational systems related to the 5 senses, they are:

Sight	Visual	V
Hearing	Auditory	A
Feeling	Kinaesthetic	K
Smell	Olfactory	O
Taste	Gustatory	G

There are sub divisions within the systems. Visual contains both imaginary and remembered images. Auditory includes both imaginary hearing of sounds and talking to ones self. Kinaesthetic includes bodily feelings, touch and emotions. The most common systems used are V, A and K.

Each representational system is part of a network:

1. *Input* – The gathering of information internally and externally

2. *Thinking/processing* – mapping, learning, decision making, motivation strategy, storage of information, memory and visualisation of the future.

3. *Output* – How we express ourselves to others through language, voice and physiology.

As individuals we have very different representational systems. If you ask a group of people who recently holidayed together to describe their recent trip, one person might talk about the view from the hotel and the glorious sunsets (V), a second may talk about the sounds of the birds and repeat stories told by fellow travellers (A), whilst a third may express how they felt with the sun on their body and the sand beneath their toes (K)

Understanding Ourselves First

Understanding how we personally use our own sensory representational systems is the starting point for our own development. It helps us to recognise our strengths and where we differ from others in communication style. Understanding the importance of this is the first step in communicating with impact.

Practice Point 2

So, let's explore to discover your own preferred or natural representation system. Take out a recent written document that you've completed and read through it. Knowing your system will be very useful in how you communicate with others.

What type of words do you regularly use? *Take a set of highlighter pens and highlight any phrases or words that belong in one of the 5 sensory groups. Use a different colour for each group. When finished you'll have a better idea of what representation system you use to make sense of the world.*

To get you started some examples of commonly used phrases below?

Visual

I get the picture, I see what you mean, let's get this in perspective, it appears that, show me, the focus of attention, looking closely, a blind spot, it's clear to me, a different angle, he's a dark one, there's a cloud on the horizon, this is the outlook, with hindsight, he'/she's shortsighted, you'll look back on this.

Auditory

That rings a bell, we're on the same wavelength, lets talk about it, who calls the tune, within earshot, lets discuss things, I'm speechless, shout from the hilltops, people will hear you, this silence is deafening, it's music to my ears, word for word, in a manner of speaking, turn a deaf ear.

22

Kinaesthetic

He/she's thick skinned, a cool customer, I grasp the meaning, a heated argument, I will be in touch, I can't put my finger on it, they are a cold fish, a warm hearted person, we are just scratching the surface, let's dig a bit deeper, he was tickled pink, she's a smooth operator, hit the nail on the head, you'll get a shot, luke warm attitude, I feel it in my bones.

Gustatory

It's a matter of taste, lets chew it over, it's a bitter pill, that's an acid comment, I have a thirst for knowledge, He/she's a seasoned pro, tongue in cheek, paying lip service, let's get down to the nitty gritty, variety is the spice of life, hungry for more and it leaves a bad taste.

Olfactory

He was fuming, it's a bit fishy, a nose for news, smell a rat, the sweet smell of success, blowing in the wind.

Knowledge Quiz 1

This is for fun and intended to help you explore your current level of understanding for the content and integrate what you've learned so far.

On a scale of 0 – 10 where would you currently rate yourself in relation to effective communication within the following areas? (please circle the corresponding number below)

Within your **family**, how effectively do you communicate with your Parents? Your Siblings if you have them?
1 2 3 4 5 6 7 8 9 10

Your Children if you have them?
1 2 3 4 5 6 7 8 9 10

And, Your extended relations and family members if you have them?
1 2 3 4 5 6 7 8 9 10

Within your **work** setting, how effectively do you communicate with your colleagues?
1 2 3 4 5 6 7 8 9 10

Your boss or superior if you have one?
1 2 3 4 5 6 7 8 9 10

And your clients if you are client facing?
1 2 3 4 5 6 7 8 9 10

How would you rate your communication skills **online social** media?
1 2 3 4 5 6 7 8 9 10

And, finally what about your **offline social** skills, how effectively do you feel you communicate with your peers when face-to-face?
1 2 3 4 5 6 7 8 9 10

Explain in your own words what Effective Communication means to you and how being an effective communicator will improve your current working environment and/or personal life.

What percentage of your communication is verbal (what you say)?
(Please circle the correct answer)

55%   38%   7%

What percentage of your communication is Non Verbal?

What are the 3 keys to effective Communication?

I.

II.

III.

What are the 5 representational systems?

1.

2.

3.

4.

5.

Give 5 examples of language for each of the 5 sensory representation systems

Visual

Auditory

Kinaesthetic

Olfactory

Gustatory

Time to complete your learning journal sheet for this chapter they are located at the back of this book.

Chapter 2

Effective Communication Is So Much More Than Just Talking

Chapter 2 ~ Effective Communication Is So Much More Than Just Talking Where you'll discover the true power of the senses and how to use them with your 6 mental faculties

Aim of this Chapter:
Is to give you the underlying technical information and practices you need so that you can apply them at will to recognise another's representation system and meet them in their model of the world for a more effective communication. I'm sure you've been in situations where both parties wanted similar outcomes but just couldn't agree on how to get there? This module will help you avoid those loggerhead situations.

Objectives of this Chapter:
By the end of this chapter you should be able to…
- Easily recognise and match another persons representation system
- Understand what is meant by the terms rapport, pacing, sensory acuity and eye accessing cues
- Analyse the combination of sensory and mental faculties being used by another
- Complete written play sheets, learning journal for marking and commentary

We have a lot to cover in this module so lets get cracking. In Chapter 1 we briefly covered what happens in the Dance of Communication and representation systems, here in Chapter 2 we'll be taking a deeper dive into HOW that dance occurs in a much more technical way.

Introduction
We'll be exploring how information is stored, processed, recalled and how your physiology impacts all interactions and how to change it if necessary.

We'll also be taking a more in depth look at your natural representation systems so that you can be more effective during your most important conversations Much of the work in this module is based on the early work of Dr Richard Bandler & John Grinder who developed a way to codify language and behaviour which they called Neuro Linguistic Programming.

Before we dive in, **take out your learning journal and complete the first section.** What's your intention for this chapter? What do you really want to get from this chapter? How will it help you in your work/life? We'll return to it later on at the end of the chapter to fill out the remaining sections.

The 3 principles for an effective communication
How will you know if the communication was well received in the way you intended? You'll be much more effective if you take these three principles to heart and live them from now on.

1. **Know your outcome**
Whether you are communicating with a person or a group you are more likely to be effective if you know what you are seeking to achieve. It helps to make your outcomes positive, specific and in the same direction as the other person.

2. **Open up your senses**
The only way that you can truly know whether you have conveyed the message you intended is to be aware of how it has been received by the other person. Their internal thinking and feelings will show in their external behaviour. To understand how people respond, notice their body position, breathing, skin colour, eye movements, hand and feet gestures, facial expressions and changes to tone and quality of their voice.

3. **Be flexible**

29

To be an effective communicator, always act on principle that *the meaning of the communication is the response it receives.* Communication is a loop. What you do influences the other person and what they do influences you. If in observing their response you find that you have conveyed a different message than you intended, take that as useful feedback and change the way you communicate in future until you get the response you desire.

The dance of communication
A large percentage of the population believe they are victims of circumstance and use excuses as stories to explain away the reasons why they have no control over a situation or the way people react to them. The trouble with this way of thinking is that it places the power to create experiences outside of our selves. If during a communication you find that people just don't respond the way you'd like them to, you may find this section most helpful. An understanding of 'The law of cause and effect,' puts you firmly in control of creating your experiences.

Cause   and   Effect

C > E

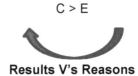

Results V's Reasons

Understanding that ALL responses we receive are caused by our actions, whether they are verbal or non-verbal and knowing we have the ability to change our actions so we receive a different response can be a great comfort.
If we use the statement: **The meaning of the communication is the response it gets, then...?**

30

What this statement does is put the emphasis firmly on you, the person wanting to get the point across rather than saying that the other person must be stupid because they didn't understand what you meant. It gives you the opportunity to say it again in a different way, to clarify your meaning and to give the other person another way of understanding what you really mean.

In his book, 'How to win friends and influence people,' Dale Carnegie has outlined his 6 principles for influencing others and they are: 1. Be genuinely interested in other people. 2. Smile. 3. Remember a persons name is the sweetest most important sound in any language. 4. Be a good listener, encourage others to talk about themselves. 5. Talk in terms of the other person's interests. 6. Make the other person feel important.

If we work with principles 1 and 4; and showed genuine interest by listening first to understand the other persons communication style, not only will we learn a great deal about that person, we will also in the process hear the words they use. When responding we can then reflect back their language patterns and words, which will be much, more effective than you ever thought possible. It will also give the other person the gift of being listened to and 'feeling understood,' which is very powerful and never to be underestimated.

Practice Point 3
Practice 'listening to understand'
In your next conversation listen out for the process words the other person is using, are they visual, auditory, Kinaesthetic, gustatory or olfactory? A vital skill for effective communication is listening to the words/language used. This is the surface structure of a communication where the person you are communicating with displays their preferred

31

representation system for taking in and storing information.

Every time someone asks us a question or makes a statement to make sense of the information we go inside our heads and search for something that matches what has been said, cause and effect. If we have nothing that matches, then we act confused. If we have something that matches or is similar then we may ask clarifying questions. Of course this is done in fractions of a second. There are ways in which you can tell where a person goes when, 'inside,' these internal communications can be tracked by an observant individual. You probably already do some of this but on an intuitive level rather than conscious one.

Understanding others communication styles and How they represent & store information

"An effective communicator joins others where they are in their models of the world"

We store information much like a computer does, but we are not taught how to store the information for recall, so when a situation arises where you need to think on your feet or come up with a response quickly it can be difficult for some people. It doesn't mean there is anything wrong with them, it just means they store and process information differently. Can you imagine if you had no system for storing your files or documents on your computer how difficult it would be to find the right file quickly?
It would take time, right? It's the same with our minds.
We all have a perfect mind!

Every person builds a different model or map of the world that is developed using his or her sensing organs of: - sight, hearing, feeling, taste and smell. However it would be impossible to take in everything that is presented to us and therefore we have our own perceptual filters, which we then use to decide what information, we take in and what we leave behind.

These filters are individual and are based on our own unique experiences, culture, upbringing, beliefs, values and assumptions. As we explore reality, our perception comes from the inside. We may think we perceive reality, but we are in effect creating our own personal reality, which may be very different from that of other people.

A useful way of thinking about this process is to compare it with map making. There is a territory; the map helps us to make sense of it however, maps are selective, and the type of information in them varies according to their purpose. For example an AA road map may be very different from an Ordinance survey map designed for walkers.

It is important to remember that '**the map is not the territory it describes'**
It is simply a representation of it at that moment in time.

We can control our personal map-making by changing our filters. Narrow, impoverished beliefs will lead to dull, limited maps. The very same world can become rich and exciting if we change the filters through which we perceive it.

It is also important to remember that every person will have very different maps of the world to you. If you said the word 'beauty' to a group of people one might see far off mountains and another a sandy beach and yet another their lovers face. There is no end to the variations on the differences of representation. There are as many variations as there are people on the planet, each individual has a way of storing and recalling information based on their unique experiences.

There are three skills you can develop to understand another person's model of the world, so you can join them. Three ways in which you can detect very small distinctions in another's, 'internal dialogue,' which aids understanding and can only be achieved by first being in RAPPORT. Second is to track the other persons EYE MOVEMENTS and the third is to develop the skill of SENSORY ACUITY. We'll cover these in more depth and give you opportunities to practice each one, which is highly recommended. The more skillful you are at utilising these three attributes the easier and more effective your communications will be.

Skill 1, Rapport

We covered in chapter 1 that only 7% of your communication is the words you use and more than half, 55% of the impact is your body language. What your body is doing during the interaction is even more important than the words you are using. If you'd like to communicate effectively then it's necessary to have the skill of RAPPORT. If you 'have rapport' it means you are in sync with them. This means that you can use your body language to show and give them the feeling of being understood. This doesn't mean you have to agree with them it's simply a sign of respect for their point of view.

We can create rapport by pacing or copying some of the other person's behavior. Then matching and mirroring their body language, voice tonality and representation system. Literally by joining them in their dance! This creates a bridge between our world and theirs; it builds trust, and is the basis of an effective communication and the basis of a long term relationship built on trust

Practice Point 4

So, to start your practice in building rapport you'll begin by pacing another person's behaviour, this is where you enter their model or map of the world on their

34

terms. It's like walking beside them at the same pace. Too fast and you'll be streaking ahead they'll have to hurry to keep up with you and too slow they'll have to hold themselves back. In either case they would have to make a special effort to stay engaged.

I'm sure you've been in a conversation with someone who speaks really fast and likewise with some who speaks really slowly and with great detail? Once you have paced another person and built rapport by matching and mirroring you'll then get the chance to begin leading them, which we'll discuss in a later module, but for now practice your rapport building skills. The art of effective communication begins when you learn how to pace another person's communication style.

An example of some of what you can match and mirror in another's communication

Body	**Voice**
Posture	Volume
Facial expressions	Tone
Hand movements	Pitch
Eye movements	Tempo
Breathing	Descriptive words
Movements of feet	Repetitive phrasing
Body shifts	Using their words exactly
Spine angle	
Head angle	

Be subtle though! Don't obviously copy every movement otherwise people might think you're a bit weird!! After you've practiced this exercise several times you'll find that you naturally mirror the other persons behaviour.

Practice Point 5
Next time you are out, watch people talking in restaurants and shops, can you tell who is in rapport and who isn't?

35

Practice point 6
In your next telephone conversation, begin by matching the other persons voice – talk at the same speed, with the same volume. Notice the quality of the conversation. When you want to end the conversation, mismatch. Talk more quickly and loudly. Can you close the call without saying bye?

Skill 2, Sensory Acuity

Scientists have discovered that during any conversation or interaction our bodies make minute changes from moment to moment. These changes are very small and are important to notice while building rapport. Developing your sensory acuity or awareness allows you to track subtle changes in breathing, skin tone and colour. This level of sensory awareness helps us to read more accurately the non-verbal signals from another person. Enabling us to develop the flexibility to change our communication style to match the other person dynamically.

The way to do this is to develop your peripheral vision. If you drive a car you already have already developed your peripheral vision. If you have children you too, will have already developed a heightened ability in using your peripheral vision. It's the eyes in the back of the head thing!

In a communication you can take mental snapshots during a conversation using your peripheral vision, this gives you information on how the person filters information in their model of the world so you can join them there. There are five main areas to track while you are listening.

1. Skin colour can change from light to dark
2. Skin tones can go from shiny to matt
3. Breathing rate can change from fast to slow and be deep diaphragmatic or shallow breaths

4. Lip size can change from thick to thin, or lines can disappear and even the colour can change
5. Eyes can be focused or unfocussed, and the pupils can dilate or undilate.

Practice Point 7
During the next conversation you have, develop your peripheral vision and sensory acuity while talking and after review it by making notes of what you noticed or became aware of in your learning journal.

A quick exercise to check your understanding of peripheral vision or check that you have it is to look forward, keeping your eyes forward raise your hands at your sides with your arms outstretched in line with your shoulders.
Keep looking forward but slowly move your hands forward until you can see them without looking directly at them. This is the field of your periphery vision. You can actually see what's happening off to the side even without looking at it directly.

Here's an overview of representation systems and how they all fit together when combining eye movements with other non-verbal communication

	Visual	**Auditory**	**Kinaesthetic**
Eye movement	Defocused or up to right or left	In the middle	Below the midline usually to the right
Voice tone and tempo	Generally rapid speech, clear tone of voice	Melodious tone, often resonant at a medium pace. Will	Low and deeper tonality, often slow and soft with many pauses

		often have an underlyin g rhythm	
Breathing	High, shallow breathing in the top part of chest	Even breathing in middle part of chest	Deeper breathing from abdomen
Posture and gestures	More tension in body, often with the neck extended. May also present with a thinner body type	May display rhythmic body movemen ts, head may be tilted to side. Often medium body type	Rounded shoulders, head down, relaxed muscle tone. May gesture a lot or touch.

Skill 3, Track Eye Movements

It is possible to identify a persons thinking process by tracking their eye movements during a conversation. We tend to move our eyes according to which representation system we are accessing. In most cases this is a reliable indicator of how a person is thinking. Although you would always be wise to test first before making assumptions because there are always exceptions.

We generally look upwards when we are accessing visual thought processes, look ahead for auditory and look down for Kinaesthetic. It is important to remember though that different people do have different eye accessing systems.

There are further distinctions that give clues to the inner processes that are being used.

If the person is looking straight this could signify that they are visualizing
If they are facing you and looking up to the left – they could be visually constructing an image and if looking up and to the right they could be remembering images.
If they looking to the left they could be constructing sounds, whereas looking to the right they could be recalling sounds.
If they are looking down and to the left they could be accessing bodily feelings and sensations and if looking down to the right they could be having an internal conversation.

Some people think mostly in language and abstract symbols. This way of thinking is called 'digital' a person processing in this way may have an erect posture and often with their arms folded. Their speech is prone to being monotone and they'll speak in terms of facts, statistics and logical arguments.

All though these examples are the most common, some people may have a reversed pattern.
Remembered images are usually on the right hand side and feelings down and to the left.

When a person visualises, they see pictures in their minds. Some people think they cannot visualise or that they do not create images. This is not the case, everyone creates images, whether they are aware of it or not. Without the ability to make mental images, you wouldn't be able to recognise your car or your house. Recognition involves matching what you see with a remembered image. If you had no remembered images you couldn't recognise familiar things in your life. The storing of images is automatic and happens largely unconsciously and very fast.

Be careful to avoid describing people as their representation system, the five systems are capabilities and preferences rather than identities.

Your 6 Mental Faculties
To help you make sense and meaning of your experiences you have also been blessed with 6 mental faculties. These faculties are what differentiate us from the animal kingdom. They are the tools that make us human and give us the abilities to choose our path and make decisions. Discovering the process of combining your 5 senses with those of your 6 mental faculties gives you unlimited power to communicate more effectively.
You already know that there are 5 sensory ways we take in information through our senses. Visual - using our eyes. Auditory - using our ears; Kinaesthetic - using touch; Gustatory - using our taste organs and olfactory - using our nose.

You have naturally taken in information using your senses all your life to date. And you may believe that the physical senses are all there is. This isn't the case. In addition to your physical senses you have 6 mental faculties that help you take in, process, recall or store information. They are, in no particular order the:

Reason,
Perception,
Imagination,
Intuition,
Memory,
Will,

The reason you probably aren't aware of these is because they function predominantly from the sub conscious mind. I can guarantee you have used them but you may not be consciously aware of using them. The human mind is capable of holding 7 + or minus 2 bits of information at any one time, which leads us to genralise, delete and distort what we take in with our physical senses to fit with what we believe about the world.

The 6 mental faculties help you make sense of your world when using your physical senses and its important to understand exactly where they come into play. Your mental faculties control your behaviour and enable you to change things in your mind. They can also be likened to muscles, mental muscles because the more you exercise them the stronger they become within you. Before we get into what the 6 mental faculties are it would be a good time to discuss the mind. Where is it located? No one has ever seen a mind but they have seen the brain. The brain is not the mind, which can be confusing so to clear up any confusion I'd like to share with you a simplified way of understanding the mind that my mentor Bob Proctor shared with me.

Dr Thurman Fleet from San Antonio, Texas, who was very interested in the healing arts in 1934, realised that to treat a person successfully he needed to treat the whole person. Not just the body but also what was happening in the mind too. Now you may be wondering why I'm telling you this, but all will become clear. There is a simple method for understanding how the mind works that will greatly help you to become a very effective communicator.

You have a conscious mind and a sub conscious mind; you also obviously have a body.
Your conscious mind has the ability to accept or reject ideas and can reason either deductively or inductively. The sub conscious part of your mind only has the ability to accept and is totally deductive.
Your conscious mind is your thinking mind and your sub conscious mind is your emotional mind. When you make a suggestion to someone using words, gestures or writing they process it using images according to

their preferred system. Associated to those images are emotions, those emotions cause feelings which in turn drives the response or resulting action. The mental faculties are used to make sense of what the physical senses take in.

This means that when I hear something, I can make it mean something totally different to the intention by the other. That meaning is developed according to my beliefs, values and preferences. So you can now see what is physically happening when you communicate with another and how important the intellectual faculties are?

Lets explore the 6 mental faculties then
To recap then, they are: -
1. Reason
2. Will
3. Memory
4. Imagination
5. Intuition
6. Perception

1. Reason – This is the one we most use to 'think' with. We mostly use inductive reasoning based on cause and effect. Mental activity is not thinking. We have a constant stream of chatter going on in our heads, this is not thinking, it's just noise which for the most part we take no notice of. The late Dr Ken McFarlane was quoted as saying, 2% of people think, 3% think they think and 95% of people would rather die than think. Thinking can be hard work, however for those who are willing to train themselves to think constructively there is tremendous compensation.

All great ideas begin in the mind. The chair you're sitting on. The pc you're using and even putting a man on the moon, all began with someone actively using their reasoning faculty and constructively thinking.

Every new idea triggers even more ideas, that is just the way of the world.

The average person who works full time, which here in the UK is roughly 40 hours a week, has roughly 6,000 waking hours, 2 thousand of which are spent at work. This leaves 4,000 waking hours of relatively free time to do with what you want. Now, I know that if you have a home or children there are chores to do, but even so if you just committed one hour a day to fully realising your reasoning faculty and developing your thinking skills you could potentially transform your income and change anything you choose to something more desirable.

If we did we would never be saying, I can't, or be at the mercy of circumstance, ever!

Practice Point 8
Test this idea for the next 30 days
Pick one hour during the day that you could commit to developing your reasoning/thinking faculty. Make it a time when you are at your freshest and your mind is clear of distractions. During this hour take a completely blank sheet of paper and at the top of the page write your present of primary goal, make sure it is clearly written.

Then write down as many new ideas as you can for achieving your goal. Keep going until you get to at least 50 new ideas. Now many of the ideas wont be usable but all it takes is one great idea to totally revolutionise your world.

Imagine what you could achieve if you committed to completing this exercise daily. Even if you only managed 20 new ideas a day, 5 days a week, which is only 260 hours a year and amounts to an amazing six and a half 40 hour working weeks devoted to developing your skills as an effective communicator.

Can you now see how easy it would be for you to improve every area of your life this way?

If you feel you are already overstretched test this out. Get up one hour earlier every day for the next six months and focus on ways you could improve your working environment. You'll be astounded at the difference it makes to every area of your life.

2. WILL - Lets now look at the WILL, Nothing can ever be achieved in life if there is NO WILL to achieve it. **The will gives us the power to choose**. As human beings we have been gifted with the power of choice and free will. We have the capacity to choose what we think about and how we represent events.

The will, when focused gives us the power to cut out all distractions and remove resistance. Have you ever experienced a time of intense focus? A time when you have been so engrossed in what you are doing that time flies past? Or even where physical time feels like it's passing so slowly, 10 minutes feels like an hour and you can't wait for it to end? Your will or your power to choose drives these responses. If your mind is elsewhere, time passes slower than if you are 100% involved in the activity and totally present.

We have the capacity to choose and decide how we view a situation. If for example you have a meeting with someone who has a different representation system to you it could easily degenerate into a clockwatching nightmare, if you don't have the tools and skills you are developing in this course. The challenge with being disengaged means the conversation often ends in one or both of you feeling disrespected and misunderstood. The will enables you to focus your attention and concentrate on the other person and ensure that you both feel the benefit of the interaction.

Practice Point 9

44

A simple exercise that you can use to train your will is to sit in a darkened room with a lighted candle. Stare at the candle flame while relaxing your gaze. If any thoughts pop into your head – just let them pass, don't judge them or comment on them, let them go. Do this for about 15 minutes every day and you'll find that you will be more easily able to concentrate for longer periods, allowing distractions to pass you by. This is our challenge when communicating – staying engaged without going off in our heads on a thought trip.

3. Imagination – Our imagination is the place where we create images, we create them on the screen of our minds from both real events and ones that we make up using a combination of our physical senses and mental faculties. **What we think is reality is really only our own version of events created in our own imagination**. As we discovered when learning about the physical senses we noticed that every individual has their own model of the world or the way they perceive reality. Using our imagination we have the capabilities to create full blown movies or segments using our physical sensibilities.

Everything that exists in the word today was once an image in someone's mind. They created a picture of what they desired and using the will focused their attention on using their reasoning faculties to make sure the image became a reality.

Many people mistakenly believe they don't or can't make images in their mind. This is simply untrue, as we have already discussed when exploring the physical senses. If you didn't make images you would not have the ability to recognise anything, which would make it very challenging to go about your normal life. So that you really learn the skill of visualizing I'll share with you a simple technique that will help you understand how you personally do.

45

Practice Point 10
Find a trusted partner and ask them to help you in relation to developing your skills in visualisation. On the sheet marked additional resources there are three check boxes. Get someone you trust to ask you the questions based on two experiences, one positive and one negative. This way you can utilise this knowledge to change the way you store/represent certain events and use it to help other do the same. It's especially useful to pre plan a positive outcome for everyone involved.

4. Intuition – Everyone possesses this skill, YES, even you. In recent years neuroscientists believe they have actually located the place where we 'feel' our intuition. (see, Vol 2/issue 1, New Scientist, The Collection)
All of our mental faculties are used in conjunction with our physical senses and intuition is no different. We use our intuition to read minute signals in the environment and from the people we are with. Primarily this was developed as a survival mechanism from a time when staying safe was a matter of survival and the difference between life and death. It was a very important part of our primordial brain development. Most people have been trained not to trust their intuition and I've found this seems to be a source of some confusion as to whether one should rely on one's intuition. Sometimes intuition is known as 'gut feeling' or a knowing.
In communication we are able to, 'feel' if someone is telling the truth or not. Our Intuition is triggered by non-verbal actions that don't necessarily match what is being said. Intuitively we recognise this incongruence. To be congruent simply means that your words match your behaviour. For example, we might say yes while shaking our heads, instead of nodding. Or we might say yes and then step back at the same time which in turn causes our bodies to vibrate in resonance or dissonance with the other person. It can be challenging

46

to find the words to articulate these feelings but suffice to say they are an important or even critical part of any communication.

Practice Point 11
Think of a time when you had a 'feeling' that something wasn't quite what it seemed. Replay the event in your imagination and look for the non-verbal cues displayed either by you or another. This will give you vital information on how you currently interpret non-verbal cues and the types of cues you respond to in a totally unconscious way. Practice during the next 12 conversations too.

5.Perception – Perception is our version of reality. We use our perception along with our other mental and physical faculties to create our models and maps of the world. This is not in fact reality – BUT OUR VERSION OF REALITY. Our version based on our individual filters, interests, beliefs and values. As you are already aware two people can have a totally different viewpoint on the exact same event.

For example, when I was studying Spatial Design at Chelsea College of Art & Design, we had a brief for completing a photographic project in Camden, London. We were to photograph the areas that interested us for an art installation we were to design. We were to present our images along with images of our designed installation.
My photographs showed, rough sleepers, graffiti, rubbish in the canal and derelict buildings. One of my colleagues photographs were of a beautiful tree lined canal with people enjoying themselves. The two sets of images couldn't have been more different and one would never have believed they were taken in the same location on the same day. This is the power of perception.

Both were true representations of what we saw on that day based on the filters we were using. The filters are our interests, beliefs and values.

Practice Point 12

A great way to side step or become consciously aware of your filters is to replay a recent conversation in your minds eye. Put yourself in the other person's shoes or position. Imagine you are them for a minute. If you have to do this physically, then do it. Sometimes standing in the same space, in the same pose helps us access the information more easily.

Think of a recent conversation you had with someone that ended with both of you unsatisfied with the outcome. Using your reasoning skills, think of the event from the other person's perspective. You may have both wanted the same outcome but were using different terminology to explain it. What would you do/say differently next time to ensure that both of you felt that you had been listened to and understood? Remember that you have already understood that the meaning of the communication is the response it receives.

6.Memory – YOU HAVE A PERFECT MEMORY; it is your recall strategy that lets you down. We are not taught at school how to remember and recall information, so for many it's a haphazard affair. No one has a problem with remembering things that are important to him or her.

Your memory is like the executive controller, it runs the show and helps you to focus on current and relevant information. For the average person their mind can only consciously hold 7 +/- 2 bits of information at any one time. Our brains are receiving billions of messages happening at any one time. So to prevent us from being overloaded our mind filters the events and messages around us by our interests and so everything that is considered irrelevant is deleted, distorted or generalised. This is so we can focus solely on what we

48

feel is relevant in that moment. This doesn't mean that you are unaware of the other messages; they are stored in your subconscious mind. The messages that seep past your conscious awareness become subliminal messages. These are messages that have been noted and stored on a sub conscious level but you consciously have no awareness. I'm sure you've had times when someone has asked you for information about something you haven't experienced but you know where and how to get it!!! This is simply because the information has been noted and stored in the 'that might be useful one day mind file.'

Science has proven that you can improve your cognitive abilities and increase your ability to remember information by using a brain entrainment program that involves a regular practice. This is exactly how habits are formed.

These 6 mental faculties work in a symbiotic relationship with your five senses so that you make perfect sense of the world according to your current interests, values and beliefs. Knowing this empowers you to facilitate communicating effectively with compassion so that every one wins.

Knowledge Quiz 2
Please complete your answers in this section. They are intended to help you explore your current understanding of what we've covered in this chapter, helping you to integrate your skills and practice.

Activity

1) **Explain in your own words the 3 principles of an effective communicator**
2) **Explain in your own words how the law of cause and effect impacts your communication?**

3) What are the 2 most important skills of an effective communicator and why are they the most important

4) Compile a list of words and phrases for each of the 5 sensory representation systems you heard during your practice session. (These will be invaluable to you)
   1. Visual
   2. Auditory
   3. Kinaesthetic
   4. Gustatory
   5. Olfactory

5) Explain in your own words what is meant by Model of The World?

6) Explain in your own words what is meant by Rapport and its purpose?

7) Give 7 examples of how one can build rapport to communicate more effectively?

8) Give an example of the usage of sensory acuity and why you would want to develop this skill.

9) When thinking about eye movements, generally speaking which side would you expect to see the eyes move if a person was having a conversation inside?

10) **When thinking about eye movements where would you expect to see eyes move to when the person was remembering an event?**

11) **When thinking about walking on a sandy beach where would you expect to see the eyes move to?**

12) **When thinking about hearing a favourite tune, which direction would you expect to see eyes move?**

13) **What are the 6 mental faculties?**

14) **In your own words explain the importance of combining the physical senses and mental faculties**

15) **What will you do differently in future communications?**

Time to complete your learning journal sheet for this chapter; they are located at the back of this book

Chapter 3

The 7 Vital Components Of An Effective Communication

Chapter 3 ~ The 7 Vital Components Of An Effective Communication

Aim of this Chapter:
The Aim of this module is to give you an appreciation of the underlying technical information and practices you require to develop a framework for developing and perfecting your own effective communication style so that you can apply the 7 vital components for an effective communication

Objectives of this module:
By the end of this Chapter the reader should be able to…

- Clearly demonstrate the 7 components of an effective communication and why each is important
- Appreciate and demonstrate the positive impact that a well formed outcome has on communication
- Recognise and understand the driving force that determines all outcomes
- Complete written play sheets, practice points and learning journal for return and commentary

In this chapter we are going to take a look at the 7 vital components that go towards making an effective communication. We'll be looking at it from both sides, that of the communicator and the beneficiary of the communication. I call them a beneficiary because if we begin all communication with a positive frame, that is with a win win attitude then everyone benefits. We will be covering attitude in this module as one of the 7 vital components.

Before we dive in, **turn to your learning journal sheet for this chapter and complete the first section.** What's your intention for this chapter? What do you really want to get from this chapter? How will it help you in your work/life? We'll return to it later on at the end of the chapter to fill out the remaining sections.

When communicating effectively you will have a sense of ease and positive expectancy about you and be naturally displaying these 7 vital components. I prefer to call them operating principles. Your focus will be on the other person or people and how you can give them the best possible experience while you are in each others company, what is commonly known as a win, win, win situation. As a result, you get what you want, the other party gets what they want and the world is a better place because of it.

The 7 vital components of an effective communication are:

1. **Outcomes** ~ It's important to consciously know the purpose of your communication, what do you really want?
2. **Attitude** ~ Your inner attitude is displayed in your actions
3. **Flexibility** ~ Ensuring a win ~ win will always get you what you want
4. **Framing** ~ Working from the other persons view of the world and helping them to hear what you are really saying
5. **Motivators** ~ Understanding a persons key motivators will give you the best way for your communication to be understood and really heard
6. **Increase** ~ Leaving all parties in a better place as a result of your interaction and delivering more value than expected
7. **Trust** ~ The other person and all that makes them who they are and how they can support you to reach your outcomes

We'll now take a deeper look at why each of these components are important in your communication efforts to you are more effective when it comes to getting you point across and support the other persons highest ideals whilst doing so.

1. Outcomes
What do you want? - The result is an outcome.

If you were to ask the next 100 people you meet, 'what do you want?' You are more likely to be told about all the things they don't want. Most people never think about what they do want in any real or constructive way. The most common approach by far, is to think of what one wants or believes they could have, and then quickly come up with all sorts of stories, excuses, and reasons why they couldn't actually have what they really want! This is usually because they either lack self-confidence or mistakenly believe they must know HOW to get a thing before they can dream of having it! Growing up some people are taught that it's rude to ask for what you want, or worse they may have been told, 'ask and you don't get,' or similar.

All outcomes are journeys from where you are to where you want to be. In communication all interactions are essentially a journey, a journey from one outcome to another. An effective communication usually involves the act of moving someone from his or her current position or point of view to a different position or point of view.

By setting an outcome we become aware of the difference between what we have and what we want. Only when you have set an outcome and are clear about the destination, can you then plan for the journey. The more positively you can define what you want the more likely you are to achieve it. We do this by ensuring that our outcome or desired goals are well thought through and clearly defined.
It is important to put what we want from the communication into a positive frame. A positive frame is something that benefits both you and the person you

are communicating with; it offers a solution rather than a problem. What this does is empower both you and the other person to take responsibility for achieving the result.

On the journey between moving a person or group of people from their current view to your desired view; you'll require some additional resources but you won't know what they could be until you are clear on the outcome.

Keep in mind that the other persons first interest is naturally to be inside their heads asking themselves, what's in it for me? So be very clear at the out set that what ever you say and do ensures that this question is answered first. This allows the other person to hear you better.

The best 4 questions to ask yourself before you prepare for an important communication are,
"What is the purpose of this communication?" this is the end goal, what do you want as a result of your interaction?
The second question to be clear on is, **"Why is this important to me?'** What do you want out of the communication?
And thirdly, **"How will they (the other person or people) benefit from the interaction?"** Why would it be important to the other person?
And finally, **"How will you know you've achieved the desired result?"** What will they do as a result of your interaction that is measurable to you?

Practice Point 13
Think about an upcoming presentation or important communication that you have booked and explore the possible outcomes for that event. Brainstorm your thoughts. Take out a large sheet of paper and write a title at the top of the page, then in the center write the first question. Then around it write down all the possible

answers to the question. Think of as many responses as you can, even the ones that may seem a bit absurd, just write down everything that pops into your mind. Repeat this process for each of the four questions.
At the end you'll have a practical list of words and phrases you can utilise when composing written or verbal communications.

If you can connect your desired outcome to something that the other person also desires then there is a higher chance that the other person will be moved into action and do exactly what you've asked them to do.

2. Attitude

Attitude is one of the most commonly used and yet most misunderstood words in the English language. Growing up we are told to change our attitude but never told HOW to change it. By the time we get to the end of this section on attitude you'll have a really good understanding of why your attitude is ONE of THE most important aspects of an effective communication and how to change it for the better if need be.

You would think that something that holds so much power in our lives would be taught from our very earliest age. Yet if you were to ask the next ten people you meet what attitude means, you will probably also get ten completely different answers. When you have a clear understanding of what attitude means and how attitudes are formed, it will become very apparent that only a small percentage of the population are really in control of their attitude. In truth their attitude is being controlled by the media and by other people along with the conditions and circumstances of their lives.

Your attitude defines how you experience the world. Your attitude is made up of your thoughts and feelings about the way you experience the world. So you can see how important this is for developing your skills as an effective communicator.

Your attitudes about your experiences drive your behaviours and thoughts, those very behaviours and thoughts determine your results. What this means is, if you believe that something will turn out bad, it invariably does. And if you believe something will turn out with the best outcome, it also invariably does. Henry Ford was once quoted as saying, *"If you think you can do a thing or you think you can't, you're right."*

The greater impact is that the attitude we display is usually the one that gets reflected back to us by the circumstances and those around us.

"It is our attitude towards others that determines other's attitudes towards us." Earl Nightingale

What this means, is that because everything operates on the law of cause and effect, everything we say or do will cause some effect. We discussed this in a previous chapter. Ralph Waldo Emerson an American philosopher wrote in depth about the natural laws of the universe and the law of cause and effect in the 1800's and he called the law of cause and effect, the law of laws. This shows up for us as, Good attitude = good results, fair attitude = fair results, bad attitude = bad results.

William James of Harvard once said that the greatest discovery of his generation was that, "HUMAN BEINGS CAN ALTER THEIR LIVES BY ALTERING THEIR ATTITUDES OF MIND," this means that if you changed your attitude about the person you intend to communicate with to a more positive one, then the results you achieve will be a more positive one. It sounds so simple, doesn't it? But, the challenge for many of us is how to exactly do that?

To develop a good attitude towards others we must first develop a good attitude towards ourselves. We can't give others what we don't have. It's the attitude we take towards ourselves which determines our attitude towards others. When you experience someone with a poor attitude to others, you can be sure they have a poor attitude towards themselves. They don't like themselves or they are unhappy about something. A happy person reflects their happiness in their attitude.

A person with a poor attitude most of the time is unhappy with the way their life is, and are experiencing frustration most of the time, they are often a human magnet for even more unpleasant experiences. When those unpleasant experiences come, as they must, because of their unpleasant attitude, they reinforce their poor attitude thereby bringing more and more problems! I'm sure you've been around these people? But, for the person with a good attitude, the same principle holds true in reverse, expecting the best, and that's what they get most of the time.

We've already discussed that attitude is made up of your thoughts and feelings, which in turn cause your actions. So let us first examine how your thoughts are generated.

What is a thought?
There is a creative power flowing into our consciousness. It has no form. It is neither positive nor negative. As we begin to exercise our mental faculties and give form to this power (our ideas), the first stage of attitude begins. We build either a positive or negative image in our mind. That image is expressed on a conscious level through the words, emotions and actions we then use.
When we internalise something we experience through our physical senses and then get emotionally involved with it through our mental faculties. For example when you watch a news report that doesn't really interest you, it doesn't affect you. However if there is a news report that excites your sensibilities, you are more likely

to get emotionally involved with the ideas being expressed. This is called internalising.

When an idea is internalised, we are emotionally responding or reacting to it, we are literally taking it to heart. This information goes straight into the sub conscious mind. The early Greeks referred to the sub conscious mind as the heart. In my opinion I don't think that enough emphasis or importance is placed on this aspect of how we take in and process the billions of messages that are coming at us every day.

The reason this is important to know, is because the sub conscious or emotional mind is deductive, In other words the sub conscious mind doesn't have the ability to reject anything that is impressed upon it, it is totally subjective. It doesn't differentiate between good and bad, it has no sense of humour. It is totally and completely subjective. "As a man thinketh in his heart so is he," James Allen wrote, as he completely understood this process of how internalising events impacts how we then act.

Now, why would a person persist with a poor attitude? or expecting the worst? Well, we are so familiar with ourselves that we tend to take ourselves for granted. We tend to minimse what we can accomplish or the goals we can reach. And for some strange reason we believe that others can reach heights, which we cannot! We tend to overlook the fact that we have an enormous pool of untapped potential within each of us that we habitually fail to see. There are millions of people who are currently living dark, narrow and frustrated lives; they are living defensively because they take offense, blame others and live from that defensive view. Added to that they have a doubtful attitude towards themselves and life in general so that is often their physical experience of the world.

Attitude is a reflection of a person, what is happening on the inside is what they experience on the outside. This is where you appreciate just how powerful the combination of your physical senses and mental faculties are. You have the ability to retrain your self to create positive images in your imagination. All It takes is to focus, using your will by being persistent and patient in training and developing your more powerful attitude as an effective communicator. It can bring about marvelous results.

Now, for a minute let's look at how successful and effective communicators operate. These are people who sail through life, they get on with those around them and they seem to go from one success to the next with ease. Others seem to go out of their way to help them achieve their goals and If something should occasionally fail they simply shrug it off and continue. No matter what a person does, where ever you find a person doing an outstanding job and getting outstanding results, you'll find a person with a good attitude to life.

These people take the attitude that they can accomplish what they set out to achieve. That achievement is the natural order of things and there is no good reason on earth why they can't be successful. They have a healthy attitude towards themselves, their lives and the things they want to accomplish and as a result they often achieve remarkable things and come to be viewed as lucky, confident and successful.

When you have an important communication to deliver it is worthwhile to invest the time to think of all the reasons why you can have what you want, and the benefits that the recipient will receive as a result of your interaction. Remember our environment, the world we create around us, is really a mirror of our attitudes. And **if we don't like what's happening around us, then all we have to do is change our attitude about**

it. We already have all the resources within that are
required to change our attitudes.

Practice Point 14
*This exercise could take you at least 21 days to master.
For the next 21 days you'll find yourself transitioning to
the happy, successful and lovely to be around kind of
person that everyone just loves to help.*

For the next 21 days,
> **"Treat every person you meet as the most
> important person on the earth while you are
> with them."**

*Do it from the perspective that they are here on this
planet doing the best they can. Do it from the
perspective that you are already in possession of the
success you desire. Do it from the perspective that this
is the way that human beings are supposed to be
treated. Do it from the perspective that by treating
everyone you meet this way, we form an important
habit. There is nothing in the world that men, women
and children want and need more than self-esteem and
the feeling that they are important, that they are needed
and that they are respected. They will give their love,
their affection, their adoration and more importantly
their support to help you achieve what ever you want.
Go test it out for the next 21 days until it becomes your
natural way of being.*

Practice Point 15
*Think of someone with whom you have contact with but
don't get on too well with. Now ask yourself these
questions:
How is their reaction to me, a direct result of how I act
towards them and have acted TOWARDS THEM in the
past?*

*If you have been experiencing negativity ask yourself,
How quickly might it be possible to reverse those
responses to each other?*

*Imagine for a moment, how you might be if you were
functioning as if the other person was doing their best
with the resources they currently have available to
them?* **Until you can see it in your mind you cannot
attain it as a result,** *so allow yourself to wonder what it
might be like, even if you don't have it right now. What
could it be like if the relationship improved further?*

The easiest and most effective way of developing a
good attitude habit is by conducting yourself as though
you already have a good, positive, expectant attitude
towards life. If you've never tried it you'll be amazed at
what happens. Remember, actions trigger feelings, just
as feelings trigger actions. Cause and effect. You must
first become mentally involved with the idea of being a
successful effective communicator and internalise this
as an image in your mind. Goethe a great German
philosopher said, *"Before you can do something, you
must BE something."*
We are now going to cover what BEING FLEXIBLE in a
communication means and the power it brings to that
communication.

3. Flexibility

We all have the same capability to be flexible in the
way we communicate with others. The art here is to be
able to respond from a place of understanding and
appreciation rather than reacting from a place of
aggression and fear. Being flexible in the way we
communicate enables us to calmly listen to the other
person's point of view and then reply in a way they can
understand so there is a positive outcome for all parties
is achieved.
What gives us the flexibility to communicate effectively
is the ability to hear with all our senses and faculties.
You see, many people listen but they don't really hear

what the other person is displaying. As previously discussed, during a conversation most people display all sorts of useful information about how hey store and represent information to you.

Combining the words, tonality and body language you have a way of seeing exactly what the other person is saying about the way they make decisions, the way they store information and the way they process information. For example, if a colleague was to ask you to help them with a decision, you would realise they had already made the decision, but have been putting off the execution!

Always be considering what's important to get across in your communication?

Practice Point 16
In the next conversation you have with a colleague or family member, practice being flexible in the way you communicate. Test your new skills in rapport building and changing your preferred communication style to that of the other person. See if you can match their style without being caught!!!

4. Framing
Framing the conversation or putting the communication in context is important because nothing has meaning except the one we give it. Information does not exist of its own! William Shakespeare noted that, *"There is nothing good or bad, but thinking makes it so"*
For us to receive understand and make meaning of any communication or conversation it must be understood in context. For example, if I said I saw a man cut another with a knife, should I call the police? The answer would be yes, if I saw it in the street and no, if I saw the event happen in a play, film or operating theatre. The context or setting in which the event or conversation is happening also gives us important clues about how to respond.

65

Making Meaning

In our daily use of language we distort and genralise much of what we want to communicate using labels that are in common use. For example I could say something like, 'put it on the table.' And in the room there is a dining table and a coffee table, both are tables so which one do you choose? This is the problem with communication; we must ensure we've fully understood what is being said rather than making assumptions. Our spoken words are metaphors for our inner world. Which in turn is a metaphor for our experience. We have already discussed much of this in the earlier chapters. When we meet or talk with someone we make meanings of what is important to us. In a group each member will make a different meaning of the exact same conversation

The meaning we make of our experience depends on the context frame we apply. Think of it in terms of photographs or pictures. When we look through the viewfinder of a camera we frame the picture within by enclosing it in a small frame compared to its surroundings. Communication Frames are like a viewfinder or picture frame, they surround a moment in time according to our current paradigms and beliefs. (Paradigms are another way of saying set of concepts or thought patterns.) We are always setting frames for the conversations and communications we have with others. Most of the time we don't even realise we are doing this. Understanding communication frames is an important part of knowing how to effectively communicate with others so they really hear what we intended to communicate rather than what they may think they hear.

The communication frames you decide on governs the questions you ask about what happens, how you feel about it, how you react to it and how you deal with it. Questions are a powerful way of setting the context of a frame because they include assumptions based on your beliefs about an event. For example think about these two questions and the responses based on your current level of understanding.

1. In view of the widespread anger about this subject, what are your thoughts about it?
2. Many people are angry with this, how can you help them?

Can you see how powerful, carefully framing your communications can be?

If your intention is to get another to do something you ask of them, then context frames are really useful.

Practice Point 17

If you think back to the last sales conversation you had, when you purchased a major item for your home and asked yourself the following question;
Would you have compromised on safety for a cheaper model?
Probably not!

Context frames are important because they set the point of reference by which we judge how to make a decision based on the information in front of us. The assumptions contained within the frame determine how the recipient of the communication responds based on their own beliefs, values and assumptions.

Practice Point 18

For example how would you answer the following questions?
if you had £4,000 in your bank account, would you accept a 50:50 chance of either losing £800 or gaining £1400?
Or, Would you prefer to keep your account balance at £4,000 and accept a 50:50 chance of having either £3,200 or £5,400?

Which one did you choose? As both outcomes are exactly the same, the only difference is the way the question was framed. If you are like many people then you would've automatically said no to the first one and yes to the second one, simply because the second question put the gains and losses in context of your overall finances. Giving you more information in a context that made much more sense to you.

Single words such as, obviously, unfortunately, you have… we have… they… can all be used to lead the communication in a certain direction by framing the context.

Different frames for different results
When listening to another person you'll begin to realise that there are many, many ways to 'frame' a communication, but if we listen carefully we hear the contextual frame being used. We are going to explore the language used in just 7 contextual frames, they are the:
The Big Picture Frame
The Results Frame
The Restate Frame
The Difference Frame
The Possibility Frame
The Relationship Frame
The Agreement Frame

So, lets explore each one and it's specific use.

The Big Picture Frame
This frame focuses on the long-term view or the big picture. Inviting us to look through a wider lens than usual. It encourages exploring and anticipating the possibilities and consequences beyond the normal space and time boundaries considered. Examples of Big picture frame questions would be: How would this…. change over the long term? Who else would be affected? What would they think?

The Results Frame

This frame focuses on the desired result and encourages positive action towards that desired result. It's a valuable frame to use if you already know the outcome you desire and would like the other party to emotionally buy into those same results. Examples of results frame questions would be: What are we wanting to achieve? What do we want from these specific actions? What can this do for our organisation? What can this do for me?

The Restate Frame

If you want to check that you've fully understood a particular point that has been said, you can use this frame to restate the key points using the other persons words, tonality and body language. People choose one word over anther because that word represents specific meaning in their thought processes. By restating the key words back with the same emphasis you can ensure you have understood the right meaning. The choices of words used are significant because we may have a different meaning attached to the same words. This frame allows you to check you have really understood the communication. An example of questions that could be used is: Can I check that I fully understand...? So you are saying...?
This enables both parties to ensure that the communication is being understood in the way it is intended.

The Difference Frame

As human beings we are blessed with our thinking faculties, so able to make small distinctions about how one thing compares with another. Using this comparison method we can ascertain whether one route is better than another. Using the difference frame gives us the opportunity to explore and quickly gather relevant information to make informed decisions. Example questions for the difference frame are: How is this different? What is it that makes... stand out? What are the important variations?

The Possibility Frame
This frame enables us to explore possibilities ahead of time by utilising a lets pretend approach. Beginning with an outline of a hypothetical scenario and then asking questions that explore all possibilities, both positive and negative we are able to gather valuable information about potential challenges and pitfalls. Anticipate risk factors and find positive solutions to existing problems. Example questions for the possibility frame are: What might it be like if...? Can we guess what would happen if...? Can we suppose that...?

The Relationship Frame
This frame as the name suggests evaluates the relationships and interconnectedness of a specific elements, rather than the scenario by exploring how the factors combine and affect each other. Using this frame facilitates a closer inspection of each element and it's impact. Examples of relationship frame questions are: How does this fit with what we already know? How does this connect to the wider system? What if we changed one element? What would be the relationship between these two events?

The Agreement Frame
An individual using this frame is evaluating and seeking agreement. Use of this frame brings all parties to a higher level, big picture agreement on what can be achieved by assuming that each party desires a positive outcome and that the relevant resources are available. An example of an agreement frame question would be: What can we agree on?

Practice Point 19
During the next few days begin to notice the context or frames used during your conversations. Test each frame to bring about a positive change.

5. Motivators

Every individual has a unique and very personal set of drivers for their behaviour. It is largely unconscious. This behaviour is based on a combination of their experiences to date and their natural propensities. If you take the time to watch people then it is extremely easy to begin to understand the motivators that drive them to display the behaviours they do. According to scientist Abraham Maslow in his 1934 paper titled, 'The theory of human motivation.' Where he concluded that there are typically 6 basic human needs, which in turn form a hierarchy. These desires and motivations are displayed in the words we use and the actions we take. First lets look at what the basic human needs are according to Maslow's research.

Maslow's Hierarchy of Needs Diagram

Starting at the foundation of Maslow's model we have **Physiological needs**, these are the needs of the body for shelter, clothing, reproduction and food – the basic essentials for human existence and survival. The next level up is **Safety needs** and the requirement to be safe from harm or fear of death and destruction. When this level is met we then naturally progress up to the next level, which is **love and belonging**. Connection with others just like us forms part of our basic survival mechanisms. It is very important to human beingness; it helps us make sense of the world around us. Every individual must progress through each of these stages, which forms the basic foundation of our societies and cultures.

Once each human requirement has been met we naturally move up the scale to **Esteem needs**, which are very different to the first three, as these are not essential for human survival but they are great providers of the intrinsic value we feel we personally bring to the world. Esteem needs are the requirement to feel valued and respected by others and ourselves. The next level is that of **Self-Actualisation**. This is simply that we are living or working towards our full potential. A person who is self-actualised is expressing their creativity daily and making a difference in the world. There is one more level, which is **Self-Transcendence**, it is when a person has developed their emotional intelligence to a point where they have enough resources and are no longer just concerned with just satisfying their own personal needs but become focused on societal contribution through altruistic or philanthropic means.

Within each of the above levels there are further distinctions to be understood. When we look at certain behaviours we can see that some people prefer to have variety while other require certainty to function well. There is also a marked difference between the behaviour of a person who longs for and thrives on connection to that of a person who thrives on significance. People fulfill their individual criteria within each level in a variety of ways based on the meanings they have made from their life experiences or expectations. Tony Robbins calls these, "*The 4 needs of personality and the 2 needs of the spirit.*" They are:

The 4 needs or personal		The 2 needs of Spirit
Certainty or Variety		Growth
Connection	or	Contribution
Significance		

Towards or Away Motivated?
We are always striving towards achieving something or working to avoid losing something. If you want someone to do something for you, the easiest way is to understand where he or she is functioning at now. By first listening to the language and metaphors they use

and then clarifying with them about what they want to achieve as an outcome. This action will reveal their motivational patterns and give you the basis on which to base communicating with them.

Now, we all flit between the motivators, that's just human nature, but understanding this gives you a great tool to being able to move people into action.

If you know a person is driven by fear and avoiding pain, you can talk with them in ways that supports the way they are naturally motivated, by letting them know, that by doing what you are suggesting, they will be avoiding the pain they fear. If on the other hand they are driven by a motivation toward seeking pleasure, then you can talk to them in terms of what they'll achieve and rewards they'll obtain if they succeed in what you are suggesting.

How to tell if someone is 'away' motivated? They'll be using words and phrases such as. I don't want to be broke, whereas if they were 'toward' motivated they would say; I'm looking forward to having a lot of money in the bank.

Practice Point 20
Think about your own motivations when working on a project. Are you motivated by the successful completion? By the rewards you'll receive? or are you motivated by avoiding being seen in a bad light because the project was late or missed it's targets? Think also about a recent interaction you had with a colleague and see if you can uncover their motivators.

6. Increase
Empathy and power of emotions when communicating
Impression of Increase
When you have developed the habit of treating every individual you come across as the most important people in your life at that moment, you'll begin to look

at other ways in which you can help others achieve their goals at the same time as achieving yours. By leaving them with the impression of increase you will be leaving them in a much better place than when you began your interactions with them. For example you may have been told growing up that if you haven't got anything nice to say then don't say it at all. This isn't about telling lies or being inauthentic, it's about ensuring that, if you do have to tell someone a few home truths, you do it in a way that supports them rather than destroys them. I'm sure you can readily think of a few examples where you have been on the receiving end of this type of communication. It doesn't feel very good, does it? If the other person doesn't take care in the way they communicate.

All human desire is based on the drive for increase, whether it is self-actualised or not. We're always looking forward to the next big thing or the latest gadget, this is increase in action, and if we are not increasing, we are stagnating. It's the same in the plant world; if the plant is not growing it is dying! It is always reaching for the light and we do the same. However, this desire is usually attached to getting ahead at work or buying the latest flat screen TV or some other material or personal gain!

Leaving someone with the impression of increase has a positive effect on their lives and future development as individuals. If we use praise instead of criticism we can more easily engage our fellow workers or family members to join us in our endeavors. Praise reinforces the good that people do, especially when that praise is unsolicited. It embellishes the listener with an influx of feel good chemicals to the brain and enables them to carry on achieving bigger and better results.

Practice Point 21
Your mission is:
"For the next 21 days practice delivering the impression of increase to everyone you meet."

Find something really positive to compliment every person you meet for the next 21 days. Begin the practice of noticing when others do things right instead of harping on about little mistakes they've made. You'll most likely very quickly notice that those niggly little negative behaviours simply fade away and stop altogether.

Point out the specifics of what you believe is great about the other person or their behaviour. Let them overhear you telling someone else how great you think they are and what a positive contribution they are making to your life or business. You will find that your staff, direct reports and family members will all hold you in a high esteem and begin to fall over themselves to help you out when required. This philosophy is based on the foundation, "that givers gain," coined by Jane wilhyde

7. Trust

Trust is one of those words that receive a lot of lip service whether in everyday life or in a business setting. For societies and communities to develop there must be trust. Firstly we must learn to trust ourselves to do what we say we are going to do. Only when we can trust ourselves can we extend that trust to others, trust forms the basis of ALL resilient long-term relationships. We all know what it feels like to be trusted; we carry an air of confident expectancy that we can complete all that is expected of us.

In business the level of trust is measurable by the money in your pocket. If you are trusted to complete a certain task in a business you are paid for that service, the more complex the service, the higher the pay. Trusting others to do what they excel at is a valuable skill in communication because it assumes belief in another and builds their confidence. Without trust there can be no teamwork. Whether we feel 'trusted' to carry out a particular job or task depends on what we believe about ourselves, and our capabilities to complete the given task.

Practice Point 22

Thinking about your relationships at work, what are you most trusted for? What are the main strengths that people come to you for advice on? Are you most trusted for your creativity and skills in finding unusual solutions? Are you most trusted for knowing the right person to call or always being there to help someone out? Or, are you someone that others depend on to get things done? Or, are you someone that is always asked advice on systems, processes and the fine detail? What are you trusted for?

Combined these 7 components make for a very powerful communication that has enough emotional impact to move a person to your point of view. I would recommend you, practice, practice, practice until these principles become the very nature of who you are. You have enough skills now in effective communication to meet another person from their viewpoint and build a foundation for a really strong working relationship.

In Chapter 4 we'll be exploring how to
~ Unlock The Power of Language For Effective Communication
- Understand How words change minds
- The importance of Individual motivation traits
- Discover How to motivate both Proactive or Reactive Individuals
- How to deal with Hot Buttons so every one wins

We've already covered that words only account for 7% of the impact in a communication, this means that the more concise the words, the more impactful the communication will be.

77

Using language powerfully isn't about controlling others but utilising all the resources you have at your disposal to get the best out those you work and live with.

Knowledge Quiz 3 ~ The 7 Vital Components Of Effective Communication

These questions are intended to help you explore your current understanding of what we've covered in this section of the book and integrate your practice.

Activity

1. What four questions would you ask yourself when preparing for an important communication so that you achieve a win, win outcome?

2. Now that you've had time to put into practice treating everyone as the most important person, please explain in your own words the benefits that you have received by doing this.

3. What causes the actions a person displays and why?

4. Name the 7 Context Frames and what each evaluates

5. Think about your role at work and the conversations you have with your colleagues & peers that may have not had the result you desired. Choose just one and write it out

    a) Look through what you have written and ascertain the 'frame' used by you, and the frame used by the 'other' person.

b) Now, thinking about your intended purpose for the communication, Compose 2 alternative ways in which you could have 'better' communicated your intention

6. **In your own words describe each of Maslow's 6 human needs and how they fit with the 4 needs of personality and the 2 needs of spiritual growth.**

7. **Think about the different roles you are involved in on a daily basis and list them all, and against each role make a note of at least two ways you can give the impression of increase.**

8. **Think about your personal and professional relationships, what are you most trusted for? What are the main strengths that people come to you for advice on? List them all.**

Time to complete your learning journal sheet for chapter 3 (they are located at the back of this book)

Chapter 4

Unlock The Power of Language For Effective Communication

Chapter 4 ~ Unlock The Power of Language For Effective Communication

- Understand How words change minds and influence others
- Discover How to motivate both Proactive or Reactive Individuals
- How to deal with Hot Buttons so every one wins

Aim of This Chapter

Is to give you an understanding and appreciation of how important it is to carefully choose the words you use when speaking and thinking. To raise your awareness of your own language use to a level that empowers you, so that you can choose the right words and speak without sending mixed messages that could be perceived out of context.

Objectives of This Chapter

By the end of this module the learner should be able to:
- Choose the 'right' words to speak without ambiguity
- Recognise the power of language and how to use it most effectively to encourage and empower others
- Know how to use words to resolve conflict and take the heat out of situations

Before we dive in take a few minutes to fill out the first section in the learning journal for this chapter. Keep in mind your intention for learning the information presented to you and what you really want to achieve by completing the course. Remember if you'd like a digital copy visit www.donnastill.com/resources

Words may be just 7 percent of a communication but they are very, very powerful, so having the

ability to choose them to fit any situation is a great advantage for any individual.

In this chapter we address the challenge of moving people into action without force or manipulation. Using only the power of words and in turn develop the capability to naturally bring out the intrinsic desire for others to want to assist and work with you.

Words Change Minds

Words help us create images in our minds, which in turn helps us make decisions about the actions we will take, the actions we take determine our results – So you can appreciate just how important words are to communicating effectively.

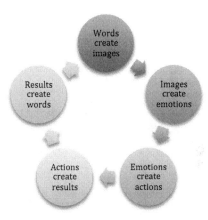

What you are about to learn are advanced techniques for persuading and motivating others. This chapter is about working with the power of language to effectively communicate to and move people into action, whether that is a child, a work colleague or a complete stranger. There will be times when clarity of speech and using the right words in the right sequence is of real importance. This chapter should give you the practice and knowledge underpinning effective communication.

The rest is up to you. By the end of this chapter you will know exactly how to use words to change minds.

You will have the advanced tools to listen and hear the myriad of clues given when another person speaks. So that you can respond with impact and motivate others to get the job done.

You will also have, a better understanding of your own individual motivation factors, your motivation decision drivers. Your own information sorting mechanisms and rule structures so that you can effectively understand what language you must use regardless of the other persons stance in the moment.

You'll find that you no longer have to deal with so many hot buttons and obnoxious people because you can hear their motivation factors and begin at once to speak in their language. You'll know exactly how to restore peace
Before we jump in,
If you haven't done so, take out your learning journal and complete the first section.
What's your intention for this chapter?
What do you really want to get from this chapter?
How will it help you in your work/life?
We'll return to it later on at the end of the chapter to fill out the remaining sections.

lets jump in.
To speak clearly without ambiguity and make your mark in the world is what we are all striving for, whether we realise it or not. Some people seem to be blessed with the gift of saying the right things at the right time so that others understand them. While others seem to feel that their voice is never heard or they are simply misunderstood. To have a voice and share it confidently is one of our greatest gifts as human beings.

Whether we are at work or at home we all need to communicate to get our point across with clarity, especially if we want someone to agree to a course of action. The more effective we are at communicating and being in rapport, the greater the chance of achieving the results we desire. Moving someone into action requires that you have an understanding of his or her operating model and that you understand what their key motivators are.

Historical Theory

Much of the way communication is taught today is based on theory initially postured by Aristotle. (According to Wikipedia) He gave us Ethos, Pathos and Logos, we'll explore briefly here because they form the foundation of all marketing activities. Take any advert or request and you'll find each of these three categories fulfilled. I expect you're wondering why I mentioned marketing?? Marketing in its simplest form is the act of persuading someone to do something they may not initially wish to comply with. If your marketing is not effective then products wont be sold and the business goes bust. We can learn a lot about persuasion from the developments in the world of marketing.

In 300BC Aristotle noticed that to get others to hear us we must appeal to three sensibilities, which we'll briefly explore below.

Ethos is an appeal to ones inner critic; by speaking directly to our credibility, our authority and our mastery in the subject. We can do this by choosing language suitable for our audience and speaking in terms of restraint.
Language to Use: sincerity, speak of fairness, accountability and transparency in a way that enables us to be compliant with the law.

Pathos is an appeal to our emotional being by conveying our values in a passionate way. We can do this using metaphors and similes. A passionate delivery conveys those values that deeply resonate within the listener by appealing to their inner emotions. Stories are a great way to engage the listener on the journey with you invoking sympathy and empathy.

Language to Use: vivid descriptive words that paint a picture with emotional narratives and connotative meaning's.

Logos is an appeal to the reasoning or rational mind, the part of us humans that require hard statistics and facts to both qualify and quantify a statement's authenticity.

Language to Use: To satisfy this part of the human psyche it requires factual date, proof-points and definitions. Literal and historical references along with 3rd party endorsements

Consider these when working through the next sections in this chapter as they give an important insight into human nature.

In summary then You already know and understand that we all use differing communication methods to covey our point and add meaning to the words we use, but how else can we find out what the other person is thinking or feeling regarding a topic we may be conversing about? With so many styles and preferences, how can we quickly find out the information we require to pick the right words and be the most effective communicator we can be?

What Does An Effective Communication Consist Of? Lets just recap here for a minute. Communication is a dance, an interaction that we've covered in depth in the earlier modules. In my view, in addition to the communication dance we also require the best version of the three core competencies for effective communication, they are **listening, language & love** to bring understanding here's why

86

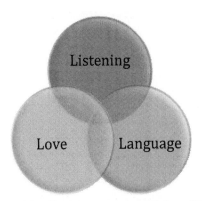

Listening with all your senses and faculties
because – without listening you'll miss out on the tonal
clues and cues that offer deep insights into the
meaning of the communication. Remember it's the
delivery that we respond most to and it amounts to 38%
of the overall communication.

Language because - the language you choose to use,
even though it is only 7% is extremely powerful used
consciously or not! Using language in an incompatible
context causes problems and sometimes even violent
responses. I expect you've been out for an evening and
witnessed just such an event. The words people
choose during a conversation tell you exactly where
they are in terms of reference to their state of being. (I
run advanced communication workshops teaching
these skills, visit www.donnastill.com to ask for an
invitation to participate) The language used displays a
snapshot into the person's world in that moment in
time. This in turn gives us vital clues in how to respond,
so they can hear you as you intended rather than have
them make up the meanings they believe you are
communicating.
Love because – to care enough about the other person
in the interaction to ensure that any resolution or
outcome is a win for all parties. By keeping this at the

heart of your interactions you'll find that you'll have no shortage of people who want to help you.

You must hold within either consciously or unconsciously an underlying love and compassion for the improvement of yourself and your fellow human beings otherwise you wouldn't even be reading this information. It's the motivation I've used to generate this information. As I believe that no matter who you are, your background, race or experience, you have something of immense value to offer the world. Our challenge is to overcome our resistance to communicating our message to the world.

Questions Are The Answer!
If you want to truly master the art of effective communication without manipulation then understanding how to powerfully use questions to get results will be a key asset to you.

For a question to be powerful it must be asked in context, with the aim of gaining a deeper understanding of the other person's individual motivation traits and value drivers, which can vary from situation to situation. We all know people who behave one way in one set of circumstances and be totally different in others. You may even find this has been your experience. You behave and adhere to a set of rules at work and yet at home you function by totally different set of rules. This is quite normal and right in most cases. There is however a core set of values that remain the same, no matter what. This is because each of us also has our very own unique set of individual motivation factors, motivation decision drivers and sorting mechanisms, which can seem totally incomprehensible for us based on our own unique experiences and filters. Questions allow us to quickly identify the best way to effectively communicate with others.

We've already discussed at length how you can begin to unpick the process of understanding others by listening to their language and watching their body language. Here we are adding an extra dimension to the mix by exploring, how asking powerful questions impacts the outcome of a communication, So that we can reduce the time it takes to effectively communicate our message.

It is universally understood in sales processes that questions are a request for more information. When someone questions you, do you come from the position of, they are simply requesting more information rather than criticising? Depending on the context we might offer further info or get angry!

The Power of Questions
Questions give you the opportunity to know what's going on in someone else's mind. Questions have the power to direct a conversation and gauge interest. Questioning skills also give you the tools to help others understand why they've been asked to do a certain thing in a certain way.
Questioning techniques give you the ability to help an individual overcome fear or rejection and completely reframe a situation so that fearing judgment becomes a thing of the past.

An example I use in my workshops is – *imagine you are asked if you like a thing? You want to say no, but something inside you says, yeah! It's ok! You don't want the other person to begin questioning you because you don't want to hurt their feelings. What do you do?* I always turn to questions. I ask them questions about the topic, about themselves about their hopes and aspirations for the topic so that I can find a way to frame the response in a way that is helpful for them – rather than just saying yes or no!! Obviously there are situations when time, conditions and question framing mean you must just give the quick answer regardless of the outcome.

Practice Point 21
Imagine you are a project manager and you need feedback from your team to move the project forward. You value their input and you want to guide the conversation to a certain outcome – namely, by the end of the day you must have a plan! You want to elicit everyone's input regardless of their preferences and motivation systems.
Where do you start*?*
Getting others to share opinions freely, if they are not naturally inclined to do so can be a challenge. With the skills you have so far, what questions would you use to enroll them into your course of action? This will be your base point for the next section.
Make a note of the enrolling questions you'd use taking into account your personal experience of your work colleagues. Doing it this way helps you integrate the information in this chapter.

One of the resources I find useful in this area is the Kolb 4Mat System, great for questioning without confrontation.

4MAT 4 Success Questions
Framing your questions based on the type of knowledge you require makes logical sense for most people to be able to get involved in the activity. Combine this way of using questions with an understanding of others learning styles and you will have a profound affect on your communication. Encouraging another to give their opinion or input in a non-confrontational way is very powerful. There is a large body of work developed originally by David Kolb, Phd. The table below is an outline of where specific questions fit in the original 4mat model.

Kolb 4Mat

Remember; give yourself the space to practice the techniques to a level of mastery – where it becomes automatic for you.

Most people automatically shy away from asking questions because they either don't really want the feedback or they are scared of the response they may illicit. They are happy with things the way they are and we'll cover why later in this chapter on individual motivation factors.

In a group situation if everyone is aligned to answering the same question, it's much easier to focus the group thinking processes and achieve the desired results. There is an order that I find works well:

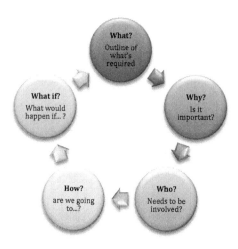

For example, if you are just beginning a new project or task it makes sense to ask 'what' questions rather than 'how' questions to begin with. How questions are analysing and detail oriented. What questions are big picture, scoping questions. What? Opens possibilities to explore options. How? Goes into the minutia, which can stifle a project in its early stages, because the how has not yet been discovered because without the what, how can you know???

Following on from the what, is the requirement to know what's in it for me? The why? If you want to enroll people in your projects its vital they know what the benefits are for them. You can only know this by having an understanding of their learning styles and language preferences.

Then, 'who? Who is going to be involved? Who it's for? Who will benefit? Who's already doing it? Etc. If it's a totally new project, knowing if there are already examples available to you is of great benefit. As is knowing who will benefit and profit from your activities.

Now we know what we are doing. Why we are doing it. Who the main beneficiaries are and when it's likely to happen, we can begin to explore how? How will the project be delivered etc.? With the information gathered in the earlier rounds of questions we can easily work out the details of HOW we can do it. The final stage is the What if...? Scenarios. The benefit is to find any holes in the plan so that it can be refined.

Do you see now how important the sequence is for asking effective questions? When this is combined with the representation systems you have a powerful way of communicating your message. Everyone get to air their views, feeling listened to and fully understood.

Practice Point 24
Time to explore and practice your skills. Someone who is very detailed, Kinaesthetic and analytical will ask a different question to someone who is a big picture visual thinker even though they may require a similar outcome. While you are at work, begin to notice the language patterns in relation to the type of questions your colleagues ask. Remember to make notes in your journal relating to this exercise.

In this section we are going to explore question types and when to use them. Firstly though, almost all question types fall in to one of 2 categories, they are either

Open Questions or Closed Questions
What is an open question and how is it used?
An open question is used to begin an enquiry and gather information; the nature of it, 'opens' the conversation to exploring the available options and possibilities. An open question will be more likely to receive a long answer with much detail and enables you to steer the conversation in a specific direction so the respondent feels they have been heard. The greatest gift we can give another.

If you want or need to find out more information, asking open questions will enable you to gather as much information as required. When using open questions encourage your respondent to share their personal opinions, feelings and experiences without judgment. If you want to find out something specific then you can ask open questions around the subject so you can build a complete picture. This formula for questioning is particularly useful to business owners, managers as they give insights into user experiences, which in turn can help you develop products and services.

What is a closed question and how is it used?
A Closed question is used to limit options, gain agreement or closure and can be answered very simply with a concise yes, no or very short answer. A closed question enables the quick generation of facts, to bring closure and the questioner remains in control of the conversation.

Below is a brief summary of open and closed questions and their usage, it's definitely not exhaustive and I'm sure you'll be able to add your own.

Open	
Example	Example
To find out what another person thinks or feels about a topic. To develop conversation To encourage sharing of opinions & experiences To explore opportunities	What would you do to improve the project? What keeps you awake at night? How you do it differently? Why have you chosen that option? Describe the benefits you perceive? Where else can we use this?

Closed	
Example	Example
Are limiting by the nature of the questions They quickly enable you to obtain facts Can be very quick to answer	If we were to have the paperwork ready would you be willing to sign today? When you have completed this task, will you be ready to move on? Do you know the answer? Are you willing to participate? Would you like help with that? How old are you? Do you live locally? Are you a member of...?

How We Make Decisions

In chapter 3, we explored individual motivations using the Maslow's hierarchy of needs. In this chapter we are going to add another layer to Maslow's research using what Shelley Rose Charvet calls motivation traits. (For further research into this her book is called, 'Words that change minds.')

Essentially, in every context we have a set of rule structures and motivation factors that drive our decision-making processes, which we will be exploring in this next section.

Please remember that Individual Motivation Factors are always contextual and very personal to each of us due to the individual application of rule structures in any given situation.

The Individual Motivation Factors
Individual Motivation Factor 1
When you master this factor you'll be more easily able to motivate people to either achieve their goals or avoid the problems they most fear more effectively.

Towards Desires V's Away from Fears
The way to recognise which direction a person is motivated by is to listen to whether they frame themselves as working towards an objective or working away from problems to be solved or prevented. This motivation factor changes according to context and where a person will be away from in one situation they may well be working towards in another. Only about 20% of the population is equally towards & away from, the rest are equally divided as definitely towards or away.

How each shows up in the world
A person who has a towards preference
In a given context, people with a, 'towards' preference will be working towards their objectives. They'll think and talk in terms of achieving their dreams and goals and be excited by their achievement and attainments. They tend to be good at managing priorities but often don't spot the pitfalls and obstacles so can struggle when it comes to identifying obstacles ahead of time.

A person who has an away from preference
Will be easily able to see what should be avoided, their motivation is triggered by a problem to be solved or when there is something to move away from. They are energised by threats and love a deadline, which really gets them into action. They are good at trouble shooting, solving problems and pinpointing possible obstacles.

Recognising speech patterns of a person with a toward preference through

> ➤ They will talk in terms of what they gain, achieve, have or get; Inclusion
> ➤ What they want, share their goals

Recognising the body language of a person with a toward preference

> ➤ Pointing outwards, head nodding, gestures of inclusion

Influencing a person with a toward preference through language

> ➤ Talk to them in terms of how being involved will be beneficial to them and the greater good; use words like attain; obtain; have; get; include; achieve; enable you to; benefits and advantages; here's what you'd accomplish;

Recognising speech patterns of a person with an away from preference

> ➤ Will mention situations to be avoided
> ➤ Will talk of unwanted circumstances and situations
> ➤ Will mention the detail of the problems and challenges

Recognising body language of a person with an away from preference

> ➤ Will display gestures of exclusion, of removing things, shaking heads

Influencing a person with an away from preference through language

> ➤ You wont have to; solve, prevent; avoid; fix; prevent; not have to deal with; get rid of; its not perfect; lets find out what's wrong; there'll be no problems;

Individual Motivation Factor 2

When you master this factor you will understand a persons decision-making process.

Internally Referenced V's Externally Referenced

The way a person decides on a course of action or makes judgments depends on whether they are internally or externally referenced. For some the decision making process is inside them and for others the decision making process is based on outside sources.

How each shows up in the world
A person who is Internally Referenced
A person with an internal reference pattern will always provide his or her own motivation from within. They decide about the quality of their work. They also have trouble accepting other people's opinions and outside direction. They don't like being 'bossed' around. When they receive negative feedback on a job they considered well done, they will question the opinion or judge the person giving the feedback.

You'll find an internally referenced individual gathering information from outside, but ultimately it is the person that makes the decisions based on their internal standards. They take 'orders' as information, which can make them difficult to supervise and since they do not need external praise, they tend not to give feedback.

Internally referenced people hold their standards within themselves for the things that are important to them. Their motivation is triggered when they get to gather information from out side and process it against their own standards and make judgments about it.

A person who is Externally Referenced
Externally referenced people need the opinions of others to know they are ok and on the right track. They require outside direction and feedback to keep them motivated. If they do not receive feedback they will not know how they are doing so they lose interest and move on to something else where they can obtain direction and feedback. They do not hold standards within themselves, they gather them from outside and

in its absence will feel like they are suffering sensory deprivation.

40% of people are either internal or external with 20% being equally both.

Recognising an internally referenced person's speech patterns and behaviour
> ➢ They say things like I know
> ➢ They evaluate their own performance based on their own standards
> ➢ They resist when someone tells them what to do
> ➢ Outside instructions are taken as information

Recognising internally referenced body language
> ➢ Sitting upright; pointing to self; pause before answering a judgment as they are listening to internal voices
> ➢ Minimal facial expression or gestures

Influencing internally referenced individual using language
> ➢ Only you can decide; you might consider; it's up to you; I suggest you think about it; try it out and decide what you think; here's some information so you can decide what to think; for all the information you just need to decide;

Recognising speech patterns of an externally referenced person, they will talk and behave in terms of:
> ➢ Other people or external forms of information will decide or judge for them
> ➢ They need to compare their work to an external norm or standard. E.g. A checklist or quota
> ➢ Outside information is taken as a decision or order

Recognising externally referenced body language

> ➤ Leaning forward, watching for your response, facial expressions indicating they want to know from you if it was alright

Influencing an externally referenced individual using language

> ➤ You'll get good feedback; others will notice; it has been approved by; well respected; you will make quite an impact; so and so thinks; I would strongly recommend; the experts say; give references; scientific studies show;

Individual Motivation Factor 3

When you master this factor you'll be easily able to identify which route to take so that leaders willing step into lead and supporters the support roles.

Proactive Responders V's Reactive Responders

The way to tell if a person is proactive or reactive is to observe whether they take the initiative on a project or wait for others to lead?

How each shows up in the world

A person who is proactive will tend to act with very little consideration and have a tendency to jump into situations with very little thinking or analysis. They'll say it seemed like a good idea at the time if questioned, what ever the outcome.

A person who is reactive will wait for others to initiate or wait until the time is right to act. They may never act. Preferring instead to fully consider and analyse the situation because they want to fully understand the situation before deciding on a course of action to follow. They'll generally be at the back of the queue, waiting!! They never seem to get started on projects and become a great source of frustration for the more proactive types. They are often extra cautious and can give you all the options up front because they really have analysed it to the nth degree.

According to research carried out by Roger Bailey about 60 - 65% of the population fall somewhere in the middle and the rest are 15/20% either side.
How to meet them in their world to achieve the best outcome and positively influence the situation?

Recognising a Proactive individual through speech patterns, they will:
> - Speak in short sentences using nouns, active verbs or tangible objects
> - Speak as if they are in control of their world
> - Use a crisp and clear sentence structure
> - Be direct and in the extreme may even 'bulldoze' their way through!

Recognising Proactive Body language:
> - May show signs of impatience, speak quickly, pencil or foot tapping and the inability to sit still for prolonged periods

Influencing a proactive person using language
> - Go for it; just jump in, why wait; right now; right away; get it done; you'll get to do it; take the initiative; take charge; run away with it; right now; what are you waiting for;

Recognising a reactive individual through speech, who will speak in terms of:
> - Incomplete sentences, subject or verb missing
> - Passive verbs or transformed into nouns
> - Lots of infinitives
> - The world controls them, things happen them, believe in chance or luck
> - Long and convoluted sentences
> - Taking it easy, about analysing, und⸍ the situation, waiting for, or the pr⸍ thing
> - Conditionals, such as could, ⸍ may and be overly cautiou⸍

Recognising reactive body language
➤ A willingness to sit for long periods of time with no urgency

Influencing a reactive person using language
➤ Lets think about it; now that you've had time to analyse it; you'll get to really understand; this will tell you why; consider this; this will clarify it for you; think about your response; you might consider; could; the time is ripe; good luck is coming your way;

Practice Point 25

Lets take a look at a hypothetical scenario to integrate this new information.

Stuart is a 55-year-old man who has always struggled with taking advice from others. He doesn't need any one to tell him though, as no one else can meet his very high and exacting standards. He now successfully runs his own business that delivers joinery services to residential homeowners and has been doing so for a number of years. There is this one job that is becoming a pain because the homeowner refuses to pay the last installment on the job he has already completed for them.

The Problem from the homeowner's point of view
Stuart gave them a very detailed quotation for the work carried out with all the expenses also outlined. The problem is that the final material costs were more than the owners budgeted for as per the original quote outline. They believe they are not liable for the extra costs and Stuart maintains it was only ever an outline. How would you deal with the situation? And what would you have Stuart tell the homeowners?

Small Words Big Impact

There are some extra words that I believe we must cover in this chapter because they are so powerful and often used to keep us locked in unhelpful language and behaviour cycles. Used effectively can powerfully form a situation into one that is of great service to ne

When we use the word: **TRY** –This is a great avoidance tool. It helps us avoid rejection, feeling bad, suffering guilt when in fact it really means that you don't believe you can do what ever has been asked of you. Often another will ask you if you can do something for them and rather than be what may be considered rude or unhelpful you'll say "I'll try," but this really means I know I don't have a hope in hells chance of doing that for you but I'm too scared to tell you the truth because I don't want to feel bad or I don't want you to make a scene so I'll humor you and tell you I'll try!

BUT is a dismissive word and is often used unconsciously to mean that everything that was said before is complete B*S*! I'll share some examples of situations where BUT is a big player and how to use it more effectively.

1. Someone else gave you a great suggestion, and you know, you either cant don't or don't believe it, or couldn't care about it so you say BUT and then follow it with your own suggestion.
2. But is often followed by the story of why you can't do the thing that has been suggested! Excuses!

When you have a person telling you all the reason why they cannot do what's requested, you can use **AND** – instead of a counter but! What this does is sidestep the story and honors the other person at the same time. By honoring their perspective you can more easily gain their trust, making them more likely to comply with your request.

Chapter 4, Unlock The Power of Language For Effective Communication

Knowledge Quiz
Please complete your to this section. They are intended to help you explore your current understanding of what

we've covered in this chapter and help you integrate the knowledge and experienced gained.

Activity

1. Please describe in your own words what is meant by each of the following?
    Ethos
    Pathos
    Logos

2. If a work colleague has a Kinaesthetic language style and you needed to let them know about a great project you'd like their help with how would you utilise Aristotle's theory when appealing to them?

3. Please state in your own words what you believe to be the power of successful questioning techniques?

4. What are the Kolb 4mat question styles?

5. You would like your team to help you create a new product or service in your business; Please state 4 ways in which you could enroll them so they enthusiastically join in?

6. What is the most productive order of asking questions when enrolling people in a project?

7. What are the two main categories of Question types?

8. Give an example of an open question and its key benefit?

9. Give an example of a closed question and its key benefit?

10. Give an example of where you have used an open question at work?

11. Give an example of where you could effectively use a closed question at home?

12. Please describe how your questioning style will be different now you have this information?

13. Please generate at least 5 questions you could use gain agreement or bring closure to a challenge or situation you've been working on using the different representation styles and questions?

14. You are the parent of a teenage son who is reluctant to complete his homework. He is very analytical and uses a lot of visual language. What would you say to him to encourage him to complete his homework if was also away motivated?

15. What would you say to him if he was towards motivated?

16. You are the manager of a busy Salon and its time for appraisals. June is a 32 year woman who is very conscientious, she really enjoys her job and takes great pride in serving her customers. The problem is, June doesn't always stick to the timings, which means that she has to make a choice between cancelling subsequent treatments or staying really late at the salon. June doesn't see it as a problem but the salon is losing revenues because of it. How would you approach the subject and help June to see the importance of managing her time

more effectively using your language skills\?

17. **How would you recognise an individual who is both reactive and internally driven? Please give at least 2 examples**

18. **Please give at least 2 examples of a sentence that could be used to positively influence them.**

Time to complete your learning journal sheet for this chapter; they are located at the back of this book
WOW!! I'm so proud of you and your commitment to your development. You now have in your hands the tools and techniques to really,

- Understand How words change minds
- Discover How to motivate both Proactive or Reactive Individuals
- How to deal with Hot Buttons so every one wins

You have shown real commitment to being an effective communicator.

Getting someone to answer truthfully may be a challenge in the beginning, as politeness often wins out. You have been developing throughout this book a comprehensive new skillset utilising all your modalities to elicit and deliver information via the other person's preferred communication style, to achieve both your outcomes. It doesn't matter whether you are an employee, manager, CEO or parent there will be many times when you require others to do something they may not want to do or like to do. You have a new skillset that will, with practice enable you to choose the right words that have people doing what you asked with pleasure.

This is one of a number of courses we offer to the small business owner who wants to get ahead and grow their business.

Diamondology – A proven six-step system for turning insights into profits. Increasing your business revenues so you can make more money by doing what you love.

Retail in the Digital Age – how to make the best use of all that digital has to offer for your retail business

Interiors To Impact – a course for retail outlets to make the best use of the retail environment to increase sales

Please visit www.donnastill.com for more information regarding any of the above or to discuss working with Donna in any way.

107

Learning Journal Pages

In this section you'll find the 4 learning journal pages to help with your development while completing the book. If you choose, you can make a note of your outcomes, what you've learnt and what you still want to develop. This way you'll be able to track your progress and more easily integrate and acknowledge the new skills you've acquired.

There are printable versions available if you email me directly at donna@donnastill.com with book resources in the title.

Learning Journal
Chapter: 1
Title: What is Effective Communication?
My outcome for this chapter
Learning points
Areas for development/Action points
Strengths

Learning Journal
Chapter: **2**
Title: **Effective Communication Is So Much More Than Just Talking**
My outcome for this chapter
Learning points
Areas for development/Action points
Strengths

Learning Journal
Chapter: 3
Title: The 7 Vital Components Of Effective Communication
My outcome for this chapter
Learning points
Areas for development/Action points
Strengths

Learning Journal
Chapter: 4
Title: Unlock The Power of Language For Effective Communication
My outcome for this chapter
Learning points
Areas for development/Action points
Strengths

Acknowledgements

There are so many people I'd like to thank for their part in getting this content onto paper and into the hands of those who it can help the most. I am deeply indebted to the help and support of the following people. Apologies in advance if I have left any one out but please be assured you will always hold a special place in my affection.

Firstly I'd like to thank Matthew Griffin, fellow TIR facilitator who's original encouragement ignited the spark for the beginning of this book coming together through an e-course developed for his online e learning academy. Bob Proctor for showing me how to remove the blocks that were previously limiting the possibilities I held for myself. Amanda Holges, the team and fellow members at Metis Women whose belief helped me see to fruition the benefits of calming/slowing down enough to focus on one thing at a time. To Yvonne Halling who introduced me to a whole new dimension and Rita Hraiz who has shown me how to open to the universal calling of my dharma. Words alone cannot express the depth of my gratitude to all of you and those who support you in the work you are doing in the world.

Bio ~ Donna Still

Exposes Hidden Opportunities
"In my experience of 30 + years working across 15 industries, independent business owners are not making the most of the opportunities available because they either can't see them or believe it will be too hard to put in a system to implement additional ways of generating automatic income." Says Donna

Every business has within, a rich stream of possibilities in terms of product and service development opportunities; combine that with immediately available insights that Donna helps them to expose and you have one of the most powerful income generating instruments accessible to the independent business owner. Diamondology is a proven 6-step system for generating a steady stream of income producing assets for your business as easily as turning on a money tap.

Some of the businesses Donna has successfully worked with have been accountants, coaches, consultants and retail outlets. With a design background, she is quickly able to work with you to map out opportunities, ensuring you, your team and your business are all operating from a place of trust, strength and adding value to your chosen market. One of the most important factors to understand is that working with Donna is not for the feint hearted, your business will not be the same after your time together. Using disruptive technologies both digital and analogue you will develop new ways of working with and serving your ideal market.

An expert in unpacking strategy and showing teams how to communicate their message more easily. Donna has been successful in helping teams tackle their communication challenges and turn their experience and expertise into profitable assets for the past 5 years.

Helping them extract the information that until now has been inaccessible by the people who needed it most. To find out how to put the Diamondology 6 step system to work for your business email donna@donnastill.com and check www.donnastill.com for events Where I'll be sharing these 6 steps in an interactive workshops for you to begin implementing in your business immediately.

The author of 6 books and 3 published training programmes Donna has worked with 15 diverse industries over the 40 years she has been working; Donna has the breadth of experience and expertise to help you help your business grow, beginning right now.

The 6 Step Diamondology System incorporates
  ➢ Designing a total product experience with the potential to disrupt your industry
  ➢ Building your team for dynamic results
  ➢ Speaking so your customers will listen and come back to spend more
  ➢ Planning for the best possible outcome

Printed in Poland
by Amazon Fulfillment
Poland Sp. z o.o., Wrocław